KU-064-690

/23

BLIND FIELD

Literature Gift Aid
£

0 031150 015255

By the same author

POEMS

The Slant Door (1979)
November and May (1981)
Short Wave (1984)
The Photographer in Winter (1986)
Metro (1988)
Bridge Passages (1991)

TRANSLATIONS

The Tragedy of Man. Imre Madách (1989)
Through the Smoke. Selected Poems of István Vas (1989)
Anna Edes. Novel by Dezső Kosztolányi (1991)
The Blood of the Walsungs. Selected Poems of Ottó Orbán (1993)
New Life. Selected Poems of Zsuzsa Rakovsky (1994)

BLIND FIELD

George Szirtes

Oxford   New York

OXFORD UNIVERSITY PRESS

1994

Oxford University Press, Walton Street, Oxford OX2 6DP
Oxford New York Toronto
Delhi Bombay Calcutta Madras Karachi
Kuala Lumpur Singapore Hong Kong Tokyo
Nairobi Dar es Salaam Cape Town
Melbourne Auckland Madrid
and associated companies in
Berlin Ibadan

Oxford is a trade mark of Oxford University Press

© George Szirtes 1994

First published in Oxford Poets
as an Oxford University Press paperback 1994

All rights reserved. No part of this publication may be reproduced,
stored in a retrieval system, or transmitted, in any form or by any means,
without the prior permission in writing of Oxford University Press.
Within the UK, exceptions are allowed in respect of any fair dealing for the
purpose of research or private study, or criticism or review, as permitted
under the Copyright, Designs and Patents Act, 1988, or in the case of
reprographic reproduction in accordance with the terms of the licences
issued by the Copyright Licensing Agency. Enquiries concerning
reproduction outside these terms and in other countries should be
sent to the Rights Department, Oxford University Press,
at the address above.

This book is sold subject to the condition that it shall not, by way
of trade or otherwise, be lent, re-sold, hired out or otherwise circulated
without the publisher's prior consent in any form of binding or cover
other than that in which it is published and without a similar condition
including this condition being imposed on the subsequent purchaser.

British Library Cataloguing in Publication Data
Data available

Library of Congress Cataloging in Publication Data
Szirtes, George, 1948–.
Blind field / George Szirtes.
p. cm. — (Oxford poets)
I. Title. II. Series.
PR6069.Z7B57 1994 821'.914—dc20 93–48951
ISBN 0–19–282387–6

1 3 5 7 9 10 8 6 4 2

Typeset by J&L Composition Ltd, Filey, North Yorkshire
Printed in Hong Kong

For László Kunos and Gabriella Fekete

ACKNOWLEDGEMENTS

ACKNOWLEDGEMENTS are due to the editors of the following publications in which some of these poems have appeared: *Critical Survey, European Judaism, Illuminations, Independent, London Magazine, Matrix, New Hungarian Quarterly, Poetry Ireland Review, Poetry Review, The Rialto, The Spectator, The Times Literary Supplement, New Writing* (Minerva), *The New Poetry* (Bloodaxe, 1993), *Poetry Book Society Anthologies* 1991 and 1992.

CONTENTS

BLIND FIELD

'When we define the Photograph as a motionless image, this does not mean only that the figures it represents do not move; it means they do not *emerge*, do not *leave*: they are anaesthetized and fastened down, like butterflies. Yet once there is a *punctum* [detail], a blind field is created . . . on account of her necklace, the black woman in her Sunday best has had, for me, a whole life external to her portrait.'

—Roland Barthes, *Camera Lucida*

AN ACCIDENT

You're simply sitting down. It's getting late.
The sky is a thick slab of premature dark,
metallic, of imponderable weight.
And noises start: a scratch, a whoosh, a bark.

Sometimes you read of accidents: a child
killed in a car, a freak wind raising hell
in an obscure American town, wild
storms of atoms raging inside a shell,

and it's like the room is just too full of you,
your senses, your own presence in the chair,
your breathing hands and feet, all pressing through
a visible integument of air.

I watch you sitting down as on a stage.
The accident begins. You turn the page.

INUIT

I have fallen in love with this baby
whose empty eyes and wrinkled mouth
appear to be essence of baby,
his death a perfect pathos
without sentiment, still as a photograph
of stillness, without potential energy,
with how he looks and does not look at me.

Could he be the Christchild under an Eskimo moon,
part moon himself with pitted eyes,
proverbial round cheese, a comforting thing
in uncomforting space, registering surprise
at the thingness of anything and everything?
And why is he more touching than any live baby?
More nocturnal, more animal? And might he wake up soon?

I hit a deer once, doing a steady lick
at dead of night. Its quivering body
was a thousand startled eyes. I didn't see him fall
but felt his dark soft leg, a heavy stick,
hammer briefly at my metal sheath
then disappear as we sped on, unable
to adjust to his appearance, or
the knowledge of his death.

It was on the brow of a hill. We were heading north,
the notional arctic, but would later bend east
toward Norfolk as the sky lightened. I want to speak light
for the baby, that he might understand. Let him at least
hear the noise of our passage over the earth
and watch the live deer crashing out of sight.

A DOCTOR'S ROOM

There was in his room an old X-ray machine,
part coffin, part phonebooth, strips of metal,
mahogany frame, leather. It was a grand house
and this the grandest room. A gentleman
might sit here waiting, whistling a little
before the heavy drapery of the curtain,
peering at pictures, or reading a magazine
by the light of the great glass.

Inside the cubicle the darkness sat
patient as a patient, till one drew
the flap aside and entered the capsule,
protected, naked, still decent,
and waited to be cut through
by the brilliant equipment
which could pinpoint organs, bones and heart
with light as hard as a jewel.

From The Wreck of the Hope to the wreck
of reason in a glass. His pictures spoke
soft landscapes to a gentleness of carpets.
His painters were personal friends
who read books, knew the psychopathology of jokes
but told them just the same, inventing new ends
to old beginnings. When they fell sick
he treated them to the latest tablets,

analysed their love affairs and cancers,
had them in stitches as they once had him.
He was growing old. A young lady saw fit
to help him across the street. He thanked her
gallantly, admired her ankles, which were slim
and tantalizing as his wife's once were,
though she was blonde not dark. Light dancers
still flitted across his hungry wit.

Of course he knew what the cubicle wanted,
what it meant when she appeared in dreams.
He was a realist. A narrow space
did not go in for ambiguity, and yet
he clearly understood her schemes
to capture him. It was something he could forget
for days at a time and then be suddenly shunted
into her arms, into her hushed grace.

He was becoming venerable, a sir to everyone.
That hard invisible light would break his bones
along with his heart and expose the frailty
of one who had prided himself on being useful.
The world of maps was tired. He was full of groans.
He found himself insufferably dull.
He would soon be seen through. The war was won.
His servant brought his boots in. Who was she?

ELEGY FOR A BLIND WOMAN

1

The house beautiful was no longer beautiful
yet high pink walls and recessed panels were gentle
and the lift was an old woman who would forget
where she was, and dark incidental

figures on landings hesitate in the sun
before doorways and kitchens with pans and bare
pipes that snaked free of walls before passing on
behind ornamental railing, down into the stair.

If there were children in apartments below
or above hers they were like pigeons that roosted
briefly on balconies. One wouldn't quite know
when they had arrived but would find them clustered

then flown, or hear—not exactly their voices—
but pittering feet and small beaks. They were
really children and elsewhere, with tangible faces
in a world quite real though invisible to her.

2

Unobserved, unadmonished, the china boy
embracing the china girl's ankle was daring,
while she, for her part, pretended not to enjoy
his attention though one could see by what she was wearing

that she was made for it. Her mother's eyes
stared piteously down at all she could not see:
letters on the cupboard, spoons on tables, dead flies
on windowsills, her hand on her own knee,

and two dead husbands, visible in her head,
the last one kindly, with large yellow teeth,
a bald, rubber-lipped darling of a man. Instead
the cassette player with its stories, the death

7

of time, the tapping about in the kitchen, the loud
coarse voice she discovered in her throat and the panic
at any small loss. She moved through a hostile crowd
of animate objects, in a darkness thick

with temper. Even her friends were impossible,
and her stethoscope fingers trembled with fury
for moments on end. Their obtuseness, the trouble
they caused not realizing her injury,

whole seconds wasted looking for words, and the kind
woman smiling piteously down, also infuriating
because unseeable, like furniture in the mind
which mind keeps moving about, disorientating.

3
She was never lovely, but once as a child
she was sent to a lycée and she returned plump,
delicious, mature, speaking fluent French,
and there was something about her skin and clear eyes

which was perhaps lovely. Later her pebble glasses
misted at weddings, froze in brutal February ice
and there never were children. The greyness set in
as everywhere in the country, with fevers, opiates,

thin chalets on the hill, a uniform dereliction.
Behind the screen children did not touch
her dangling hand, let alone kiss it. Grey
turned to black or whatever colour she called it,

red sunlight, lilac cold, sepia tablecloth.
Her brother came, glistened, fidgeted, died
like the ancien régime which seemed now almost
benevolent, rubber-faced, like an ugly child

in a house without fabulous statues or butlers,
where the sun would hesitate on the landing,
clear its throat and pass on, out of the yard,
across the green park, heading for the river.

WINDOW

Out of this single moment a window opens
and out of the lens or the gun a sadness spurts,
and all the broken glass and the spent cases,
the taps and sinks, loose shutters and other patterns
assume a statuesque pose, turn stone faces
to the present whose silence hurts
because it's sweet with the smell of distance.

The dead swim through their pictures. Their grey water
soaks our hair as we dream of where we were
while others are still fighting, smoking, posing
before buildings in an unexplored quarter
of the city and a shutter keeps opening and closing
to trap them in mere words, but our lips blur
as they meet and there is nothing left to tell.

FOR ANDRÉ KERTÉSZ

Two Aunts Appearing

An old woman in an empty square:
a man approaches her at the far corner.
It is the winter of the year after the commune.
The trees open their mouths and gasp for air.

An emptiness is working through her bones
like acid through a zinc plate, drawing
a blueprint of veins,
lost clear shapes, skin-scaffoldings.

Two heavy black aunts flap free
from under her black scarf, a generation
of brittle bones and headscarves,
part of a conspiracy

to colonize the squares and streets of the mind
with remorse. But they are tender:
their legs are thin glass monuments that sway
with the gentle nudging of the wind.

Accordionist

The accordionist is a blind intellectual
carrying an enormous typewriter whose keys
grow wings as the instrument expands into a tall
horizontal hat that collapses with a tubercular wheeze.

My century is a sad one of collapses.
The concertina of the chest; the tubular bells
of the high houses; the flattened ellipses
of our skulls that open like petals.

We are the poppies sprinkled along the field.
We are simple crosses dotted with blood.
Beware the sentiments concealed
in this short rhyme. Be wise. Be good.

Hortus Conclusus

A woman feeding geese might sit like this,
in a walled garden with rabbits and birds,
and an angel come and purse its lips for a kiss
speaking air instead of words.

And so the child was born, out of the air
and a scroll flew like a pennant to proclaim
the kingdom to which he was heir,
where everything was white and had a name.

Now languages dissolve I'll start again
with shadows, touch and sight.
I'll reinvent a world of geese whose reign
will seek new synonyms for white.

The Voyeurs

What are they staring at? Haven't they seen enough?
Perhaps it's natural to stare at backs.
Just as we pass a lighted window light makes
visible that wealth of alien stuff
of which half our minds are made,
leaving us lustful, lost and afraid.

They too are in transit. Look at his hat
(a straw boater), her headscarf (a long
inverted flame), the way their clothes hang.
There must be a hole in the wooden slat
and beyond it something perfectly new
and terrifying that light will not let through.

VOLUPTUOUSNESS

I think of a child dancing along a faint chalk line;
the sound of his feet, the flop of his hair, and his breath
a short skipping rhyme of tumbling aspirates.

The small knotted belly, the slightly sweating thigh,
the damp neck and palm, and nearby on a bench
a mother or elder sister rich in voluptuousness.

My sister is an enclosed garden. In the garden
the soft wickerwork of worm casts, black earth nipped
into buds, scored into clefts and crevices.

On windy ways a dancing underground.
Inside the bones unsettling swathes of thought,
the mind exposed to crisp surgical fingers

that pinch it into song, the local floods
of swollen veins whose banks cannot contain
their discontent. I think of my two children

swept along those waves, arriving where they are
at pianos and computers, before their mirrors,
their eyes illegible, a foreign writing.

I was once a child too, leaning over the edge of the pram,
examining my brother like a specimen, with my mother
behind the lens, her face hidden, rich in voluptuousness.

PASSENGER

A long stop at a hot provincial station.
Heat turns to dirty water, little jewels
of smut, rivulets of perspiration.

The light crowds close, concentrates in pustules,
drops of poison, off-white, plump, opaque,
suspending grit in a soup of molecules.

The trees too are hemmed in. Their heads ache
in deserted railway yards, among lines
of empty wagons in sidings. They bake

in powders, asphalt heaps, among faded signs
announcing factories with broken windows,
wreathed in smears of smoke, in the confines

of yards with scatterings of scrap iron, rows
of used flasks abandoned years ago
to trucks blocking gates that neither open nor close.

*

The girl is far too smart. Her wrists are bare,
uncluttered. She wears four finger rings,
a thin gold anklet. How clean she is. Her hair

is neatly bobbed and shining. All her things
declare a certain distance: the delicate shoe,
the lycra top, the jet black pants' rustlings

and foldings. Even her scarlet nails look new.
But not her book, the *History of France*,
an ancient faded copy. She's half-way through

and turns each page with an impatient elegance.
Despite the carriage's wild jolts and swings
the book on her knee maintains its precarious balance
and this, as Holub tells us, gives her wings.

15

FOR DIANE ARBUS

Paragons

Those with two heads know something you don't—Diane Arbus

Distrust everything—especially the happy face,
the successful face, the face with something solid
stacked behind the eyes. Locate instead the scapegrace,
the lost and the squalid,

those who have nothing to say with the eyes but the eyes
are open and inward or are lost down a well
where you look down the shaft to find them and their faces rise
like your own in the circle

of water, with lips large as dinner–plates: the man with a tail,
the man who smoked cigars with his eyes, the Siamese twins
in Hubert's or Huber's where there is neither male nor female
but paradigms and paragons

that tickle your guilt and your pity. You say: I don't want
to make you cry, but when the button's there you press it.
And it's true that those with two heads know something you don't,
only you guess it.

On a Young Lady's Photograph Album

The parents seem to be dreaming the child and the child
to be inventing them—Diane Arbus

We don't finish smaller and clearer as the years go by
but blurrier, vaster, ever more unfocused, full of grains
that dance before the face, evaporating in a sky
of rising cloud, and what remains
is perhaps a voice saying (for instance) 'mother'.
Even appearance becomes something other

than imagined, something between the atoms, like a rift
between lovers, one that must be filled with bodies or words
and a peculiar tenderness. We watch as clouds drift
behind the face, and afterwards,
as the face slowly dissolves, the contradictions
settle in to be resolved in gentle fictions

of families, of children with their pets, and of spaces
with the smell of the past trapped in their unstable walls,
of doors that open on nothing in rambling palaces
where Disney's Sleeping Beauty falls
asleep and the ivy is your mother's long hair
blown into tangles that strive against the air.

The Baths on Monroe Street

*You're carrying some slight magic which does something
to them. It fixes them in a way*—Diane Arbus

At the baths of Monroe Street two women are crying.
The walls are patched and blistered like Eliot's Jew.
Decades of steam. The carpet is wet through
with feet or with tears and the matrons are dying
of cancer or disappointment, their hair crimped in sheets,
their broad bosoms swaying over stomachs arranged in pleats.

In a sudden fury Alice begins. She launches a volley
of clicks at the mist and the leery disappearing
smiles of a hundred Cheshire Cats who may be hard of hearing
but know an assault when they see one. Like a reveille
the cry goes up to wake the dead, and the dead rise
out of the walls and the water with terrible answering cries.

Ah love let us be true to one another! they wail in the steam
of the baths, remembering their Matthew Arnold. The towels snap
as they descend on the savage intruder, the teeth also snap
and the air's full of flesh. They can see the gleam
of the lens, which is Alice in action, and they close in
as all nightmares do, on those who are rigid or frozen.

They take the instrument from her (and who after
all can blame them? Because theirs is a life not to be opened
like a tin of sardines, because they feel they own what has happened
and goes on happening to them as they totter and fall
on the slippery carpet) and by the time their energies fail
the camera is drowned in a cleaner's convenient pail.

Bichonnade

—*that we may wonder all over again what is veritable*
and inevitable and possible and what it is to become
whoever we may be—Diane Arbus

The Mystic Barber teleports himself to Mars. Another carries
a noose and a rose wherever he goes. A third collects string
for twenty years. A fourth is a disinherited king,
the Emperor of Byzantium. A fifth ferries
the soul of the dead across the Acheron. There's a certain abandon
in asking, Can I come home with you?

like a girl who is well brought up, as she was, in a fashion,
who seems to trust everyone and is just a little crazy,
just enough to be charming, who walks between fantasy
and betrayal and makes of this a kind of profession.
It takes courage to destroy the ledge you stand on,
to sit on the branch you saw through

or to fly down the stairs like Lartigue's Bichonnade
while the balustrade marches sturdily upward, and laughter
bubbles through the mouth like air through water,
and the light whistles by, unstoppable, hard
and joyful, though there is nothing to land on
but the flying itself, the flying perfect and new.

THREE CHANDLERESQUES

The Big Sleep

A perfect bubble of space floated above him.
A pool opened
at his feet and he dived in.
Eyes of glazed terracotta swam in dim
wreaths in a building like a church. What had happened
to Marlowe? Some Mickey Finn

been shot into his veins. The stillness froze
to further stillness,
the cold grew jaws.
A library like Michelangelo's
stretched its long neck before him. A stewardess
showed him through doors

into a courtyard where the statues talked
in stern–sweet voices,
an orange tree
fountained at the centre and a baby milked
its mother's breast with gentle and precise
movements while she

glanced sadly up at him with the sea in her eyes.
You're doing fine
Marlowe. Now do
the difficult thing. Get up and walk. To his surprise
the ground stood firm, longing to be defined
by his feet, so he walked through

into his own heart's aching and felt strong,
a youthful Marlowe
like a tune blown
by a child on a whistle. Then what sounded wrong?
No more perhaps than a strange voice in his window.
Maybe his own.

The High Window

White light, grey stone. That solving moment when
a thought appears
and settles on
a landscape, amplifies some hidden pattern
of trees, unscrambles the clouds and clears
the face of a pale sun.

Windows divided between transparency
and reflection,
the giving back
and the absorbing of vision, the hard currency
of what exists and what remains unknown
between white and black.

Winter sunlight on walls, light frost on grass;
the dripping distant
call of birds in leaves
in a bare forked garden behind glass,
perfect, lost, and no more important
than passing waves.

Daydreaming, Marlowe? Better than nightmare
this lit column
between annuncee
and angel, in a perspective of the air,
with blue hills, quaint flowers and a solemn
Latin delivery;

better sanity than madness, at least to be saner
than we sometimes are;
better the calm
rules of proportion, of *pietra serena*,
than the preaching of mad monks or the dictator
with his long arm.

The Lady in the Lake

Their bodies were straddled along the road:
not spartan men,
their spoils of war
were bodies taken out and spoiled, a heavy load
of shopping in a drift of plastic bags, a bargain
from the big store.

Black warriors in Pompeii skins, black holes
in further space, holed
like ships, not sinking.
One death is a thousand deaths. The rolls
of honour are full of names that grow cold.
You are thinking

too much, thought Marlowe as he waited for the car
to rise from the lake.
One death is all you need.
The face is washed away. The particular
becomes the general. Easy to mistake
the pretty head

for dough, the upper for the nether lips.
Too Jacobean
Marlowe. Consider
the fate of Marsyas whose narrow strips
of skin wailed like a high-pitched organ
over the ladder

of his ribs. Consider even that woman
filling her mouth
with pills, going down
in her holed ship, still trying to summon
the images that sank her, a truth
with which to drown.

TRANSYLVANA

for Peter Porter

'Sylvan meant savage'
                —W. H. Auden

1 VIRGIL AND THE LEADER

Our Virgil is thin. He waves a red carnation
in his outstretched hand. His mouth is sad.
Urine and darkness. Taxis hover at the station

like flies round rotten fruit. Roads being bad
we skate and bump along, juddering on scarred
cobbles, loose flakes of tarmac, past semi-clad

'seventies blocks. The driver brakes hard
as we shimmy round a tight bend then lets fly.
Here only patience is its own reward

and patience is unending, numbing, sly,
deflated, almost anaesthetic in effect,
sensations slowing up, the batteries dry.

*

The leader at the funeral. He smiles.
It's only a moment, barely noticeable
but someone notices. A moment to be filed

away, recalled twenty years later, a slight bubble
of air rising under dingy water. The teeth bared
for an instant. Then thirty years of trouble.

*

Virgil's wife is not long dead. He hankers
after her. Hence the obsessive tidiness.
Hence the old clothes queuing up on hangers,

a line of ghost wives, each in a different dress.
Hence the suitcases of old shoes, dead soles,
dead arches, metaphors of emptiness.

Waste not, want not. Words. Each word controls
a complex microsystem full of shoes.
There are housecoats, jackets, carefully packed rolls

of stockings, handkerchiefs. Someone might use
them sometime, these ritual cerements
whose buttons bless, whose broken straps accuse

the world-of-what-remains of innocence,
complicity, not knowing. The wardrobe
boxes up its knowledge, stores an intense

thickening, a denser universe. White globes
gather on shelves with the familiar stifling
smell of disease: bacteria, microbes, grubs.

*

The leader's face expands across a block,
rosier now, smoother. The leader himself expands
in vast apartments, ever more baroque,

golden, imperial, his gentle hands
stroking a child or a dog. Meanwhile
in the street, on diverse invisible errands,

two people whisper, turn to a third and smile.
It's only a moment, barely noticeable.
This too is recorded, in another file.

*

Rainy mornings. Virgil unwraps a packet
of cheese, carefully slices it and lays
it out in a pattern. He is delicate

in his dealings. He fills whole days
with wrapping and unwrapping, making neat
divisions. He must go easy, paraphrase

the given grammar of each slab of meat
in simple sentences, short words, with stops
and dashes. He must become an aesthete

of necessity. In dark empty shops
he exercises taste, brings grace to bear
on grease, on cooking oil, thin chops.

*

The leader hovers above the town in
a helicopter. Too few apartments here,
not enough concrete. Bulldozers begin

their upward climb. Floors rise in austere
towers. The rubble remains: a long ditch
fills with rainwater the colour of flat beer.

Panels drop. The lift is stuck. This is a rich
country. It has silver, gold and bauxite,
natural gas, a seaboard. It can afford a hitch

or two, a twenty-watt bulb on a winter night,
a telephone exchange like a starved behemoth
straddling an unlit street. Basically it's all right:

you can have people or food but not both.
The building stutters, blunders to a stop.
The ditches breed defiance first, then sloth.

*

It's spring. Virgil negotiates the hill
above the city, steep, up crumbling steps
with a view out over spires, an idyll

from his childhood. An orange river creeps
below him, escaped from a paintbox and spilt
across brown paper. Beside it, small heaps

of rubble wait for houses never built.
They shrink to miniature pyramids
of powder. Sunlight reveals a soiled quilt

of roofs and walls. Cars scuttle like invalids
from block to block.
                  Enough of looking down,
of light stored patiently under the eyelids,

time to look up to the spectacular crown
of the city and the vast five-star hotel
moated in mud, a petrified eiderdown

of cloud squarer than the rest, parallel
to the flat streets below, sheltering
its nightflown and exotic clientèle

of representatives (who knows what they bring
or what they take away). It can't be much,
thinks Virgil and keeps clambering.

    *

We're here to look for something, perhaps a house
buried half in the hill, with damp walls,
a jutting terrace and a long view across

the park to an artificial lake. Snow falls
on the branches and a surface of sheer ice
where a mob of skaters wheel and weave white petals

frilled with crystals, Transylvanian lace.
My mother's home town. The trees are thick with green.
Summer. Somewhere, in another place,

the skaters move to a frozen music between
the trees, performing a slow dance along the brink
of a precipice that cannot be seen

from where they are. They are lines of ink,
impossible to read now. A fountain jets
snow. The bandstand is a skating rink

full of toy soldiers. Above them the sun sets
and rises and sets again. My mother leans
on her elbows. Her brother pirouettes

across the lake. She is ill. A tree screens
the hidden steps which lead up to a hot
clear patch of sunlight. The ice queen

melts in a derelict house. A flowerpot
dangles dry stems in the porch. Where are we?
The skaters move in the distance, shot

through with dead light. Their translucency,
their quick black feet, remind me of birds.
The house says nothing, staring vacantly

into the bushes. Above it vague herds
of clouds meander like soldiers on patrol
at a border station between two absurd

countries, watching empty wagons roll
up and down the track. The skaters rise
from the pond. Families stroll

among the trees. The fountain dries.
The city is full of unshaven faces
darting round corners, quick evasive eyes.

*

Virgil leads his visitors to the only
reliable eating place in town. He smiles
with sad sharp eyes, a smile both lonely

and endearing. High summer reconciles
hill, hotel and river in an embrace
of light. Light drips from guttering, from tiles,

pours down steps, down the green carapace
of copper domes, shimmers across bushes,
tucks itself into leaves, settles like lace

on last night's puddles and webs, rushes
down streets, bursts round corners in wild beams.
Busy times. The proprietress brings dishes

of soup specially prepared. The bowl steams.
A terrace with a tree. A cabin proclaims OASIS.
Cola labels. Plastic. The whole place dreams

of order, is a kind of synthesis.
Its cheap and easy kindnesses must prove
something to someone, provide a basis

for argument, a point from which to move.

*

The leader and his wife. Pa and Ma Ubu
dealing out farts, flattening their foes
with sheer windpower. Obeah? Voodoo?

Quite unnecessary. A few hard blows
are enough. The agonies they suffer.
The leader leads by example. By the nose.

*

Virgil knows the leader's ways. He can spin
a dozen ways at once. He has a few obols
put by to pay, if need be, some local Charon

who can lay his hand on fine comestibles.
There are murky waters everywhere, forgotten
names and dates that vanish like snowballs

in the heat of circumstance, in rotten
alleyways, in little shops, inside the head,
in labyrinths with windings of frayed cotton.

Bills suffocate in drawers. The leader is dead?
The ways remain. Virgil–Theseus squints a sad eye
at the world still feeding out his thread.

*

*The ticket hall. Two bare bulbs burn. A third
has given up the ghost . . . Ghosts stand in queues
at holes. Ghosts bandy words*

*behind the counter. Successive greys infuse
a solid glass curtain. Beneath its waves two ghosts
engage in a discreet and aimless exchange of views.*

*

*The traffic lights too have given up. The dead
drive dangerously among the living. A policeman
flourishes his red stick like a decapitated head.*

*

The trams have sagging bellies. They drag their heels.
They've eaten too much rust. It takes four men
to steer them straight with four bent steering wheels.

*

When soldier meets driver he makes a proposition.
When driver meets soldier he makes a contribution
thereby maintaining both in honest apposition.

*

Two old men meet. They shake hands. One has lost
a leg. Friends of different tribes, they speak
the ruling language. One waits till the other has crossed

the road before moving back into his own ethnic
group. The other hobbles on, part of the great
majority; amiable and sick.

*

When patient meets doctor an envelope
passes between them. One offers obols
or collateral, the other offers hope.

*

The central square. The statue of the just
king (old dispensation). About him six
flags of the new salute in a strong gust.

The tiny local leader (new dispensation) kicks
his hind legs up, lets fly a leader's fart.
The old leader once kicked against the pricks:

the rough provincial redefines his art.

*

Virgil has friends. His contemporaries
remember everything, keep each other alive.
Everyone has his or her list of stories.

So does everyone else. People arrive
at individual outstations and make their peace
with consciences, authorities. They survive

as long as possible. Their numbers decrease,
their books smell ever damper, their pictures fade.
Some die on operating tables. Some piece-

meal, by stages, head downward, their bills unpaid,
their buttons undone. One falls under a train
after a drop too much, one having made

her bed and put on nightclothes. Their pain
is stored in umbrellas, overcoats, magazines
with half-solved puzzles. It remains

to be tidied up. Tidiness means
control and end. The pernickety
scuttling, the counting out of spoons,

the final indispensible dignity.

2 VIRGIL'S GEORGICS

after the illustrated calendar of Béla Gy. Szabó

January

Moonglow. Night. Ice cold.
Trees furred like bears.
The stars have cold hard eyes.
And so have bears.

February

A frightened rabbit sprints across a field.
A frosty creature, half bat, half bear,
clings to a tree. Small flowers of frost
explode in bushes, splinter in the air.

March

A woodpecker. Trees tangled.
A nail scratching on glass.
Frozen hair on a dead man.
Shadows like soft claws.

April

A narrow ambitious branch. A bud in swell.
A herb garden. A chestnut tree. Birds unroll
across the sky. In 1954
I could put my arms around the bole.

May

Poplars full of thrushes. Sky leans
on earth. The river dreams.
Shrubs light their torches. A bullfinch
sputters on a branch, bursts into flames.

June

The cuckoo counts your years. An oil green shade.
The grass sports asterisks and nipples.
The lean black water on the pond traversed
by indolent white ripples.

July

The lake steams. Grebes cackle. A distant shower.
Star responds to star. Black clumps dither
under trees in an electric storm. Thunder.
Lightning. Changeable weather.

August

A grasshopper swings absent-mindedly.
Few days left to swing.
One sharp beam of sunlight is enough
to burn his wing.

September

On my first day at school my mother cried
but I whistled at my schoolfellows.
Around my feet the dead leaves
were dancing like swallows.

October

A leaf rattles. A bough lies on the ground
like a lost umbrella. A live branch groans
under the chattering rain and feels
a sharp ache in its bones.

November

A magpie among aspens. All things
curve in on themselves, aware
of what is still to come:
province of bat and bear.

December

A TV frost. Interference. A snowflake
breaks up in a scraggy oak.
All things given over to destruction.
A gun. A joke.

BLINDFOLD

DANCING WITH MOUNTAINS

i.m. Ágnes Nemes Nagy (d. 1991)

I

Her verse was monumental. She seemed to be made of mountains.
Ottó said he once danced with her at a party
and it was all too much like dancing with a mountain.

She had a knack of creating or declaring heresies.
There were heretics in metre, heretics in stanzaic form,
but chiefly the heretics that banned or ignored her;

heretics who sentenced her friends, who sent down her husband
the critic, and when she found out that he'd been unfaithful
she ordered him from the flat on his release,

though he never deserted her, not to the end,
but called every week, helped her to edit her books,
wrote articles everywhere praising and defending her.

I met him there. He lay flat out on the sofa
because of his back, a yellowish, jaundiced looking man
to whom she had written one ravenous erotic address

she did not want me to translate, in which she wished
to devour him, to absorb him entirely. He said, Call me *te*,
the intimate form of *you* employed within genders.

She was dying the last time we met. We talked politics.
She asked me what I thought would happen and said if she voted
at all she would vote for FIDESZ, the party for those under thirty.

2

Between Becket and Rilke was the position she craved:
her diction was clear as spring water in sentences
simple and natural, referring to but beyond the senses.
Will-power held them together. Her images were engraved

or scratched (more physical this) into the ice.
Geysers, geology, trees steaming in winter, Egyptian
ceremonies. She tuned in her set. The reception
was perfect. Hers would have been a rocky paradise,

crystalline, more like a desert. She even looked
like Donatello's Magdalene but her god was different,
a beautiful martial androgyne sulking in a tent
before battle, her eyes fierce, her nails hooked,

while outside smaller poets ran yapping like the proverbial curs,
each of whom would have given a life to have written one line of hers.

FOUR SHORT POEMS FROM THE HUNGARIAN OF ÁGNES NEMES NAGY

Trees

It's time to learn. The winter trees.
How head to toe they're clad in frost.
Stiff monumental tapestries.

It's time to learn that region where
the crystal turns to steam and air,
and where the trees swim through the mist
like something remembered but long lost.

The trees, and then the stream behind,
the wild duck's silent sway of wing,
the deep blue night, white and blind,
where stand the hooded tribe of things,
here one must learn the unsung deeds
of heroism of the trees.

Statues

Statues I carried on board,
vast faces unnamed and unspanned,
statues I carried on board
to the island where they should stand.
Between nose and ear there were ninety
degrees, measured precisely,
with no other sign of their rank,
statues I carried on board,
and so I sank.

Bird

On my shoulder squats a bird
conjoined at birth, our souls allied,
grown so vast and burdensome
I'm racked with pain at every stride.

He weighs me down, he weighs and numbs.
I'd shoo him off, he'll not be shook.
He is an oak that sinks its roots
he digs his claws in me like hooks.

I hear his awful avian heart
drumming at my ear and know
I'd topple over like a log
if he were now to up and go.

Lazarus

As slowly he sat up the ache suffused
his whole left shoulder where his life lay bruised
tearing his death away like gauze, section by section
since that is all there is to resurrection.

FOR GRAHAM CABLE'S FUNERAL

Death is this Dickensian flunkey, pacing along
      in his polished top hat,
the four pall-bearers bowing to each other
      like mannequins at a minuet:
the music box starts and it's bedtime and night-time.

And the puzzle's little pieces are floating in free fall
      riding the extent
air of the body whose guy-ropes have snapped
      collapsing the tent
of inner air and it's bedtime, it's night-time.

Think how many pieces the human spore comprises,
      vague scents and sharp clauses
that never will join to assemble the semblance. The actor is
      one with his ill-timed pauses,
his script half forgotten. Here is the night-time

where only the small hard seed of being can weigh down
      the body no longer
a body, but memory of memory, the unshrinkable good
      that's the only thing stronger
than bedtime or night-time.

AT TABLE, 1964

At Schmidt's in Charlotte Street the old waiter
scuttled between tables, wrinkled as Adenauer.
The menu was opulent, the covers clean.
We ate wiener schnitzel with potatoes and sauer-
kraut chased by crème caramel, our table talk
joky–familiar or sour. We were creatures of mood,
and Sunday a family occasion, like bridge
or Monopoly, was a debt owed to childhood,
keeping track of lost time.

And lost time is what the restaurant suggested
with figures in shadows and rooms beyond rooms.
I can still taste the food in that arrested
development, the breadcrumbs rough on my lips,
and I find myself rattling on, as if I were an old waiter,
finding the whole thing funny and boring and sad.

That is the beauty of it: the poetry comes later,
shuffling up to you like a Low Church sacrament,
a grey-suited man with non-alcoholic wine,
glass concentrated in a bead of dark red,
serving for sign.

EAT GOOD BREAD DEAR FATHER

Every lunchtime they'd leave you a piece of *mignon*.
Now I can imagine the white of the paper bag
and the small yellow doily under the plate
in the afternoon half-dark. And I drag
from my memory not your room but mine
(or any room that seems to be half-dark)
to construct a world we may meet in. Here is the door
to the kitchen, here is the sideboard, the mark
on the tablecloth and the print of my thumb
on the page. Here nothing is known, everything dissolves
to noise or to music (but what is the difference?)
a music which says (so must mean) things, that solves
the pathos of cake on a saucer or the tiny
cosmic hum that rings an old woman's hand
as she moves in the kitchen like a conductor,
waving her notes into place, weaving the slender
sound of paper and footstep. We start as with lines
on a score, the *mignon* a radiance among other radiances,
with your blank childhood face and the space between lines
measuring distances.

GRANDFATHER'S DOG

His hat would sometimes precede him into the hall.
These were the bad days when everything went wrong
and the smell of leather followed him like a stray dog
across the carpet. It was a ghostly creature that slunk
about the flat, settling on chairs and cushions,
all soft retentive things would take him in,
the children, the women. The dog of course had suffered,
such was its nature, and such was theirs, the children and women.

Because failure and humiliation are unexpected
the dog was to be expected. And sometimes it haunts me,
the thought of the dog. I've seen him sniffing
at my brother's ankles. His sheer size daunts me,
his dumb perseverance. I saw him once, sitting in the kitchen
beside my mother, under her feet, at his most
persevering. He ate her slowly and left not a bone,
so I knew him to be a bitter and vengeful ghost.

And grandfather, the factory hand, was likewise eaten,
by him first, then gas, right from the beginning.
Even now as I walk through the town it is there, sharp
and pervasive, a smell of leather-tanning.

VARIATIONS ON ANGELA CARTER

I

He knows he is only an idea and not such a good one
but when he feels the black
flame in his blood his laughter sounds fierce in his mouth,
his outer skin, his shirt and his vest, hang slack

and he feels more than hears her singing in his ears.
He is thinking of her (who else) in her fields,
in her aeroplane, in her skin which is smooth,
her muscles which are tense, her neck which yields

to his breath, dissolving like a cloud which is soft,
wet, delicious, evanescent, full of strange words
which he tries on his tongue and relishes
oh years, years afterwards.

2

It is not so much in the saying
as in what a word does.
You hear it first in your mother's cooing,
in that delicate chortle, the buzz

which you feel as you touch her throat
with your pudginess, in her nipple as it roars
milk at you, in the scent of her arms as you stuff
your nose into her armpit, which is yours

and wolfish, and beyond all that, lovely,
singing with the entire self that it is,
with its history, tenderness,
self's infinite capacities.

3

The restaurant was full of seaweed. The waiters swam by
in their oriental coats. His own was as it was,
as it tended to be, a confusion of hair.
He was mesmerized by long fingers

paddling knife and fork above the plate opposite,
the shining rice as it disappeared into her mouth,
the milieu of strangers, familiars,
the electricity of truth

which, if truth be told, was puzzle and fright.
He was sitting on darkness but where
was she sitting, and who were these guests
crowded round tables? How hard it is to bear

the weight of words, to balance them on your fork,
to swallow them like fish out of water,
to test them and taste them as they come out,
gentle, neutral, sour–sweet, faintly bitter.

THE WORD HOUSE

for Clarissa Upchurch

The Word House

Here you and I are changed beyond redemption,
here we breathe doors and windows, eat
the food once prepared like a ghostly meat
for our consumption.

The past can take your breath away. You move
across the room, brittle, lithe, destructible,
and I write to hold you there in the subtle
nets that words can weave,

the words brittle, lithe, destructible.

Fugitive

She jumped clear of his clever words,
brittle, lithe, destructible,
a yellow dress in a green garden,
her eyes blue–grey–green,
her spine curved like wrought iron
under cotton, under the tight skin
and the softer, the possible
flesh. His eyes and fingers were cords

to bind her in a sentence, but she had
a monumental pathos and kept
moving. She was under
his skin and beyond it
in a place which smelled of thunder.
His arms swung at his sides, his eyelids pressed
down on his eyes, which were trapped
and delicate, the eyes of god.

The Sense of Memory

Not memories but the sense of memory,
as of a power, an enabling,
like the sun on a street with its
delicate scribbling.

To remember the sense of your beauty,
your weight, breath and movement
is enabling and powerful
as the sunlight on the pavement

which flits in and out of dark spaces in doorways
never quite filling a room that it enters
but leaving dark spaces
like pockets, like splinters.

The Word 'You'

Impossible to use the word 'you'
without you, to think of your beauty,
your weight, breath and movement,
without speaking the language

of those who have used the same words
and not for the first time:
I think of your beauty, your weight
and your breath and your movement,

I think the word 'love' with its landscape
of shadows and fires, lost rivers,
its haunted everyday objects,
its faces in windows.

We move in each other like figures
in landscapes. I think of your beauty,
the vast simple rocks of the mountains,
your weight, breath and movement.

SOIL

What colour would you call that now? That brown
which is not precisely the colour of excrement
or suede?
The depth has you hooked. Has it a scent
of its own, a peculiar adhesiveness? Is it weighed,
borne down

by its own weight? It creeps under your skin
like a landscape that's a mood, or a thought
in mid-birth,
and suddenly a dull music has begun. You're caught
by your heels in that grudging lyrical earth,
a violin

scraped and scratched, and there is nowhere to go
but home, which is nowhere to be found
and yet
is here, unlost, solid, the very ground
on which you stand but cannot visit
or know.

PORCH

for Peter Scupham and Margaret Steward

Generosity in Little Things

There is generosity in these gardens,
in the way the grass bends this way or that,
in the way birds enter and leave
almost, it seems, at random.
There is generosity in the wind as it
fizzes or mopes about the pond,
and I like the generosity of the road
that, however narrow, seems to go on for ever,
even as far as the sea
which is not too far away
and which tickles the soles
of generosity when it sees it.

There is the generosity of the peacocks.
There is the generosity of the visitor,
passarenes, fly-by-nights, exotic migrants

that settle like dust on the sills
that swirl like leaves in the porch.

The Japanese Hive

But move beyond the porch into the house
where memory is paper thin, a series
of partitions and bricked-up fireplaces.
Where are the dead men, gazing, pondering theories
of lives beyond theirs, of our lives and spaces?
What have they left? The skeleton of a mouse

the wasps' Japanese hive, fragile fontanelles
in the roof's skull, a piece of greaseproof paper
stretched across a blank pane, each one a taut
eardrum listening. From these you must shape a
resonance that fits your head, a box of caught
echoes or photographs of names that ring bells.

Doors may be shut but a head lies open to
the sky which rains down crumpled streets and faces.
There are wheel tracks running all along the room.
Crowds are pressing down the hall. They leave traces
then they disappear, swept clear by the vast broom
that must be tidying, letting the wind through.

THRENODY

for Matt Simpson

Wipe the white beard. Let it lie across his chest.
Smooth it flat and close his eyes too while you're at it.
What is history but a beard as white as this?
Gather the length gently, ribbon it and plait it.

The breath is long stopped and the words are all fading.
The air's no longer his. His was another planet—
Pluto, Jupiter—the dear one, so distant,
a spirit floating about cupboard and cabinet,

father of fathers, a well-tempered clavier,
God in the machine in the corner of the room.
Take up his name, cut it out with reverence,
and paste it on a new page of the family album.

Dry mouths and dry names, shells of dead insects,
heaps of moth-wings, beetle shards, disinfected,
no thought of flight now or crawling, they lurk
in the annals, sad husks, untongued, undetected,

in rooms of faint darkness with the sound of ghost feet
across halls of vague carpet and trousers in a chair,
in long-distance calls and buckles in the mirror,
faces of children: thick dark hair.

ISTVÁN VAS

(*1910–1991*)

1

When your best friends are taken away;
when your mentor's daughter (forbidden,
you live with her in secret) dies of a tumour;
when you're constantly hiding
and the love of friends protects you
from starvation or bullets,
and you return by secret corridors
to Byzantium not Rome,
then you'll know at times of suspicion
that all is suspicious and everyone's done time,
and it's only the wind that blows
between words not through them
that constitutes poetry,
so you practise your craft
lightly, assiduously,
and when that world vanishes
you too take care to vanish
with the beauty and intimacy
of a secret friend, tumour or lover,
sensibly, quietly, silently taking cover.

2

Candles in the window on All Souls' Day,
October wind gathering at the glass and rain
softening dead leaves. The tanks are rumbling again,
lorries are taking a whole town away.

We've been here before, whatever the season or year.
Your hesitant voice in mid-sentence, stopped in my ear.

OXFORD POETS

Fleur Adcock

Moniza Alvi

Kamau Brathwaite

Joseph Brodsky

Basil Bunting

Daniela Crăsnaru

W. H. Davies

Michael Donaghy

Keith Douglas

D. J. Enright

Roy Fisher

Ida Affleck Graves

Ivor Gurney

David Harsent

Gwen Harwood

Anthony Hecht

Zbigniew Herbert

Thomas Kinsella

Brad Leithauser

Derek Mahon

Jamie McKendrick

Sean O'Brien

Peter Porter

Craig Raine

Zsuzsa Rakovszky

Henry Reed

Christopher Reid

Stephen Romer

Carole Satyamurti

Peter Scupham

Jo Shapcott

Penelope Shuttle

Anne Stevenson

George Szirtes

Grete Tartler

Edward Thomas

Charles Tomlinson

Marina Tsvetaeva

Chris Wallace-Crabbe

Hugo Williams